SCHOLASTIC

Shoe Box Learning Centers

Addition & Subtraction

by Jacqueline Clarke

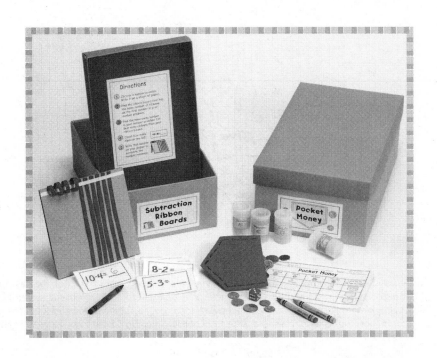

NEW YORK • TORONTO • LONDON • AUCKLAND • SYDNEY
MEXICO CITY • NEW DELHI • HONG KONG • BUENOS AIRES

Teaching *Resources*

Edited by Joan Novelli
Cover design by Maria Lilja
Cover photograph by James Levin/Studio 10
Interior design by Holly Grundon
Interior illustrations by James Graham Hale

ISBN 0-439-53794-0

CONTENTS

About This Book

It can be very satisfying to stand back and watch students using centers—working independently and gaining much-needed practice on essential skills. Yet making and storing these same centers can be time consuming, frustrating, and exhausting. This book was designed to make that process easy for teachers—and enjoyable and meaningful for students.

Shoe Box Learning Centers: Addition & Subtraction allows you to create 30 engaging, hands-on centers using inexpensive and readily available materials. Each portable center fits neatly inside a shoe box and can be assembled ahead of time, pulled out as needed, and stored conveniently when not in use. Most activities are open-ended, which allows children to repeat the activity several times during center time, reinforcing learning all the while.

The games and activities in *Shoe Box Learning Centers: Addition & Subtraction* are designed for use by individual children and small groups, but can be adapted for whole-class lessons and one-on-one teaching. As a supplement to your regular math program, these shoe box centers make it simple to weave addition and subtraction practice into the following areas throughout the school year:

- number combinations
- missing addends
- counting on
- counting back
- double-digit equations
- adding three numbers
- regrouping
- computation
- fact families
- story problems
- doubles
- counting money
- patterning

Setting Up Shoe Box Learning Centers

Shoe box centers are easy to set up and most materials are either included in this book (as reproducible pages) or are readily available at school or home. For each center in this book, you'll find the following:

- **Label and Directions:** The title of each shoe box center becomes the shoe box label—simply glue it to one side (or end) of the shoe box for easy storage and retrieval. Cut out the student directions and glue to the inside lid of the shoe box.

- **Materials:** Check here to find out which items you'll need for each center.

- **Shoe Box Setup:** Here's where you'll find simple directions for assembling each center. In most cases, all you'll need to do is gather materials and make copies of the reproducibles.

- **Tips:** These helpful hints include ways to vary and extend the activities.

- **Reproducible Pages:** Record sheets, math mats, game boards, and patterns are just some of the shoe box center supplies included in the book.

A good place to begin is by collecting empty shoe boxes, so that when you're ready to set up the centers, you'll have plenty on hand. (You might ask families to send in extras or check with a local shoe shop.) To assemble the centers, photocopy each page on colored paper (or have children decorate), and cut out the title and directions along the lines as indicated. Glue the title to the outside of the box to create a label (on the end or side that will show when you stack and store the shoe boxes). Glue the directions to the inside of the lid. Assemble and prepare any other necessary materials (such as manipulatives and reproducible activity pages) and place these in the box. You may want to enlist parent volunteers to help with this process.

Model each shoe box activity for children before having them try it on their own.

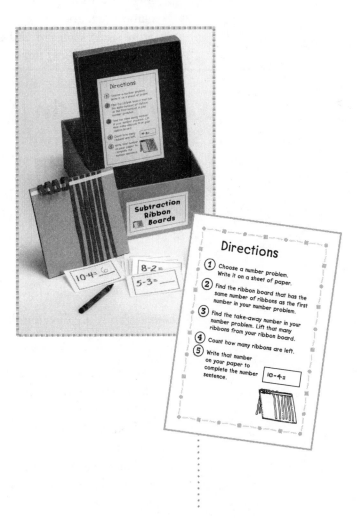

Tip

Several of the shoe box centers involve the use of number cards. To make number cards for 1–20, photocopy pages 11–12 and cut apart the cards. For other number cards, photocopy the blank card templates on page 13, fill in new numbers to make a master, and then copy and cut apart for student use. You might laminate the cards for durability. The blank card templates can also be used to create other shoe box materials, such as the equation cards for Calculate and Color (page 17).

Assessing Student Learning

To record students' progress as they move through centers, you may want to create an assessment file. To do so, provide a pocket folder for each student. In the first pocket, place a checklist of all the centers so that students can keep track of those they have completed. (See page 7 for a reproducible Shoe Box Learning Centers Checklist.) In the second, have students store completed record sheets for the teacher to review. For centers that do not require record sheets, consider using sticky notes to keep anecdotal records. Note the child's name, date, and center on the sticky note and an assessment related observation. Store sticky notes on a sheet of paper in each child's folder. Encourage students to revisit those centers where they show a need for more practice.

Meeting the Math Standards

The centers in this book support the NCTM content standard for Number and Operations, a primary focus of a K–2 math program. In particular, the activities target addition and subtraction skills, helping children to:

- understand the concepts of and relationship between addition and subtraction;
- understand the outcomes of adding and subtracting whole numbers;
- develop and use strategies for whole number computation;
- develop fluency with number combinations; and
- use various methods and tools for calculation.

Support for the process standards—problem-solving, reasoning and proof, communication, connections, and representation—occurs repeatedly within the activities for each center. For example, as children play the board game Golfing for Numbers (page 27), they add and compare two-digit numbers to move from one "hole" to the next. In the process, they use problem-solving, communication, and reasoning skills to find out who wins each hole, and eventually the game. See page 8 for a chart that identifies skills for each shoe box center.

Shoe Box Learning Centers Checklist

Name_____

Shoe Box Learning Center	Date	Comments
Bead Boards		
Eraser Drop		
Hide-and-Seek Bears		
Calculate and Color		
Cat up a Tree!		
Ten in a Bed		
Candy Count		
Give Me a Sign		
Golfing for Numbers		
Through the Zoo		
The Number Quilt		
Subtraction Ribbon Boards		
Big Snake, Little Snake		
Spot the Facts		
Ten Frame Take-Away		
Snowball!		
Picture the Fact		
The Name Game		
Seeing Double		
Doubles Addition		
Pocket Money		
Spill the Beans		
Number Train		
Polka-Dot Pajamas		
Pattern Block Pets		
Seed Stories		
Scrambled Eggs		
Name the Pattern		
Mystery Number Blocks		
Hop to It!		

Meeting the Math Standards

Shoe Box Learning Center	Understand Numbers / Understand Meanings of Operations								Computes Fluently and Makes Estimates			
	Recognize how many in sets of objects	Use multiple models to understand place value	Understand position of whole, cardinal, and ordinal numbers	Understand relationships between whole numbers	Understand relationships between number words, numerals and quantities	Understand and represent commonly used fractions	Understand various meanings of operations	Understand effects of addition and subtraction	Understand situations that involve multiplication	Develop and use strategies for whole number computation	Develop fluency with addition and subtraction number combinations	Use a variety of methods and tools to compute
Bead Boards	X				X		X	X		X	X	X
Eraser Drop	X						X	X			X	X
Hide-and-Seek Bears	X				X		X	X		X	X	X
Calculate and Color							X	X		X	X	X
Cat up a Tree!							X	X	X	X	X	X
Ten in a Bed	X	X			X		X	X		X	X	
Candy Count	X						X	X		X		X
Give Me a Sign				X			X	X		X		X
Golfing for Numbers							X	X		X	X	X
Through the Zoo	X				X		X	X		X	X	X
The Number Quilt							X	X		X	X	X
Subtraction Ribbon Boards	X				X		X	X		X	X	X
Big Snake, Little Snake	X			X	X		X	X		X	X	X
Spot the Facts	X			X			X	X		X	X	X
Ten Frame Take-Away		X		X		X	X	X		X	X	X
Snowball!					X		X	X	X	X	X	X
Picture the Fact				X			X	X		X	X	X
The Name Game				X	X		X	X	X			
Seeing Double					X		X	X	X	X	X	X
Doubles Addition	X			X	X		X	X	X	X	X	X
Pocket Money	X						X	X	X	X		X
Spill the Beans	X			X			X	X		X	X	X
Number Train				X			X	X				X
Polka-Dot Pajamas	X			X			X	X		X	X	X
Pattern Block Pets	X				X		X	X	X	X		X
Seed Stories	X				X		X	X		X		X
Scrambled Eggs				X			X	X	X	X	X	X
Name the Pattern		X	X	X			X	X		X		X
Mystery Number Blocks				X			X	X		X		X
Hop to It!			X				X	X		X	X	X

Shoe Box Learning Centers: Addition & Subtraction   Scholastic Teaching Resources

Bead Boards

Children manipulate beads to create number combinations.

Materials

- shoe box
- box label
- student directions
- scissors
- glue
- cardboard cards (about 5 by 8 inches each)
- colorful beads
- elastic cord (from a fabric or craft store)
- paper
- pencils

Shoe Box Setup

To make the bead boards, draw a line down the center of each sheet of cardboard. String different numbers of beads on strips of elastic and wrap one horizontally around each board, tying the ends together in the back. Place the bead boards, paper, and pencils inside the shoe box. Glue the label to one end of the box and the student directions to the inside of the lid.

TIP Make bead boards available at your math table for children to use when solving pencil-and-paper math problems. Consider setting up a bead board station to let children create their own bead boards. They will have fun sharing these at home as they practice more addition and subtraction skills.

Creating Number Combinations

Bead Boards

Directions

(1) Chose a bead board.

(2) Count the number of beads. Write that number at the top of a sheet of paper.

(3) Move the beads to either side of the line to create a number combination. Write that number combination (for example, 4 + 3) on a sheet of paper.

(4) Move the beads again to make and write as many different number combinations as you can.

(5) Choose a new board and repeat.

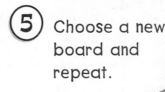

Eraser Drop

Children record the results of the game, using addition and subtraction number sentences.

Materials

- shoe box
- box label
- student directions
- scissors
- glue
- number cards, 2–10 (page 11)
- record sheets (page 14)
- colorful erasers (small size)
- small basket (or other container)
- pencils

Shoe Box Setup

Make copies of and cut apart the number cards and record sheets. Place the number cards, record sheets, erasers, basket, and pencils inside the shoe box. Glue the label to one end of the box and the student directions to the inside of the lid.

TIP **U**se small novelty erasers for this shoe box, such as those with apple, basketball, or "smiley face" shapes. Children will have fun drawing these on their record sheets, and a colorful, fun assortment will add to the activity's appeal. Replace the erasers with new shapes periodically to keep the center fresh.

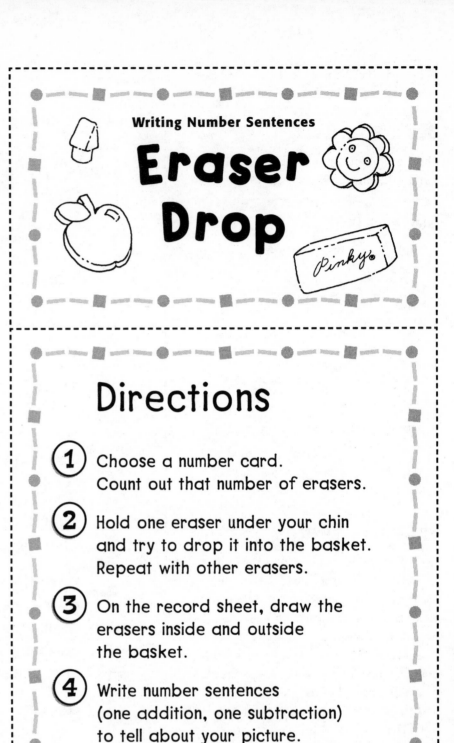

Writing Number Sentences

Eraser Drop

Directions

1. Choose a number card. Count out that number of erasers.

2. Hold one eraser under your chin and try to drop it into the basket. Repeat with other erasers.

3. On the record sheet, draw the erasers inside and outside the basket.

4. Write number sentences (one addition, one subtraction) to tell about your picture.

Shoe Box Learning Centers: Addition & Subtraction   Scholastic Teaching Resources

Number Cards

1	2
3	4
5	6
7	8
9	10

Number Cards

11	12
13	14
15	16
17	18
19	20

Shoe Box Learning Centers: Addition & Subtraction Scholastic Teaching Resources

Number Cards

Eraser Drop

Name _____   Date _____

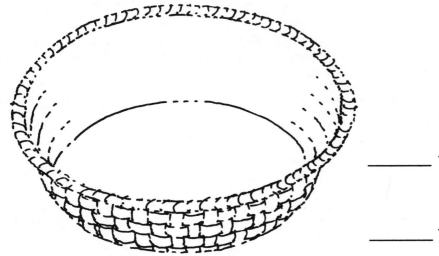

_____ + _____ = _____

_____ − _____ = _____

Eraser Drop

Name _____   Date _____

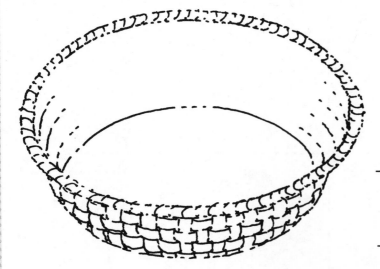

_____ + _____ = _____

_____ − _____ = _____

Finding the Missing Addend

Hide-and-Seek Bears

Children strengthen problem-solving skills and their understanding of the relationship between addition and subtraction by calculating how many bears are hiding in a cave, based on the total number of bears.

Materials

- shoe box
- box label
- student directions
- scissors
- glue
- number cards (pages 11–12)
- frosting or margarine containers (without lids)
- bear counters (or bear patterns, page 16)

Shoe Box Setup

Copy and cut apart bear patterns if not using bear counters. Place the "caves" (plastic containers), number cards, and bear counters inside the shoe box. (You may want to decorate the outside of the caves, using craft foam, construction paper, or contact paper.) Glue the label to one end of the box and the student directions to the inside of the lid.

TIP Children can develop fluency with different number combinations by using the same number of bears several times, but varying the number of bears inside the cave. Have them write equations to show the number combinations for addition and subtraction.

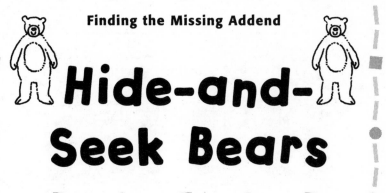

Finding the Missing Addend

Hide-and-Seek Bears

Directions
(for 2 players)

① Choose a number card.
Count out that number of bears.

② Take turns hiding some of the bears in the cave while the other player closes his or her eyes. Place the remaining bears outside the cave.

③ Ask your partner, "How many bears are in the cave?"

④ Play several times with the same number before choosing a new one.

Hide-and-Seek Bears

Shoe Box Learning Centers: Addition & Subtraction   Scholastic Teaching Resources

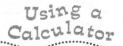

Calculate and Color

Children color in buttons on a calculator to show how they solve addition and subtraction problems.

Materials

- shoe box
- box label
- student directions
- scissors
- glue
- number card templates (page 13)
- record sheets (page 18)
- calculators
- crayons or markers

Shoe Box Setup

Write addition and subtraction problems on the number card templates. Make copies of the record sheets and cut apart. Place the number problem cards, record sheets, calculators, and crayons or markers inside the shoe box. Glue the label to one end of the box and the student directions to the inside of the lid.

TIP **F**or a variation, try the reverse. Provide calculator record sheets that have answers written in. Color in one key on each calculator to represent one of the numbers in a matching equation. Have children find the missing number and color in the corresponding key.

Using a Calculator

Calculate and Color

Directions

1 Choose a number problem card.

2 Use the calculator to solve the problem.

3 On the record sheet, color in the keys you pressed. Write the answer in the window.

4 Choose a new card and repeat.

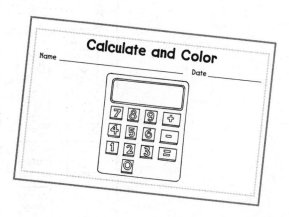

Calculate and Color

Name _____ Date _____

Calculate and Color

Name _____ Date _____

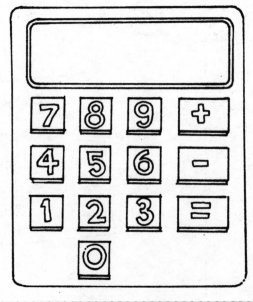

Shoe Box Learning Centers: Addition & Subtraction Scholastic Teaching Resources

Cat up a Tree!

Children explore number patterns as they race to rescue a cat from a tree.

Materials

- shoe box
- box label
- student directions
- scissors
- glue
- game page (page 20)
- timer or clock
- number cubes
- pencils

Shoe Box Setup

Make several copies of the game page. Place the game page, timer, number cubes, and pencils inside the shoe box. Glue the label to one end of the box and the student directions to the inside of the lid.

TIP **T**o vary the game, have children move up the ladder by doubling each number. This is a good way to develop strategies for number operations and lay a foundation for multiplication.

Cat up a Tree!

Directions

(1) Set a timer. Roll a number cube. Write that number at the bottom of the ladder.

(2) Add that number to itself. Write the sum in the next space.

(3) Continue adding the number you rolled to each new sum to create a skip-counting pattern.

(4) Play until you get to the top. How long did it take to rescue the cat?

(5) Roll the number cube again and repeat. Can you beat your first time?

Cat up a Tree!

Name _____ Date _____

Shoe Box Learning Centers: Addition & Subtraction   Scholastic Teaching Resources

Ten in a Bed

Children discover number combinations for ten, using bears and a blanket.

Materials

- shoe box
- box label
- student directions
- scissors
- glue
- fabric scrap "blanket"
- ten frames (page 22)
- record sheets (page 23)
- bear counters (or reduce and cut apart bears on page 16)

Shoe Box Setup

Make copies of and cut apart the ten frames (beds) and record sheets. Place the blanket, ten frames, record sheets, and bears inside the shoe box. Glue the label to one end of the box and the student directions to the inside of the lid.

 TIP Let children use the materials from this center to act out the song "Ten in a Bed."

Ten in a Bed
There were ten in the bed
and the little one said,
"Roll over, roll over."

So they all rolled over and four fell out.
Four hit the floor and gave a shout!

They kept on rolling and three fell out.
Three hit the floor and gave a shout!

They kept on rolling and two fell out.
Two hit the floor and gave a shout!

There was one in the bed
and the little one said,
"Good night!"

Creating Number Combinations

Ten in a Bed

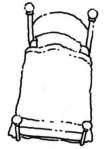

Directions

1 Place a bear in each square of the bed.

2 How many bears are there all together? Write this number on the record sheet in the first box.

3 Drop the blanket on top of the bears.

4 How many bears are not under the blanket? Write that number in the second box.

5 Solve the problem. How many bears are under the blanket? Write the number in the last box.

6 Repeat steps 2–5.

Ten in a Bed

Name _____ Date _____

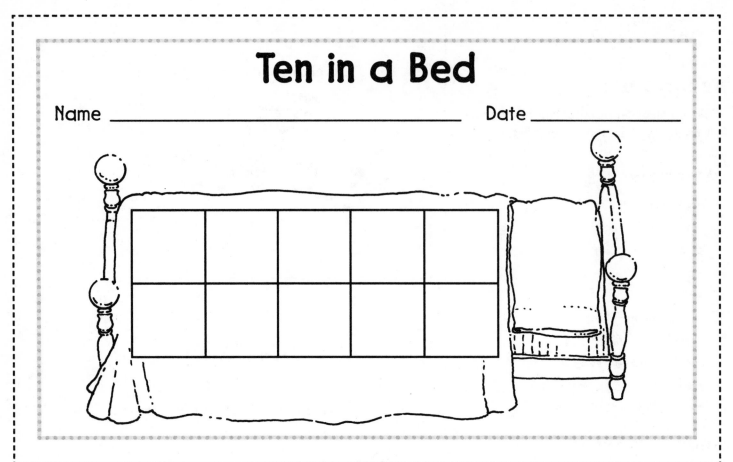

Ten in a Bed

Name _____ Date _____

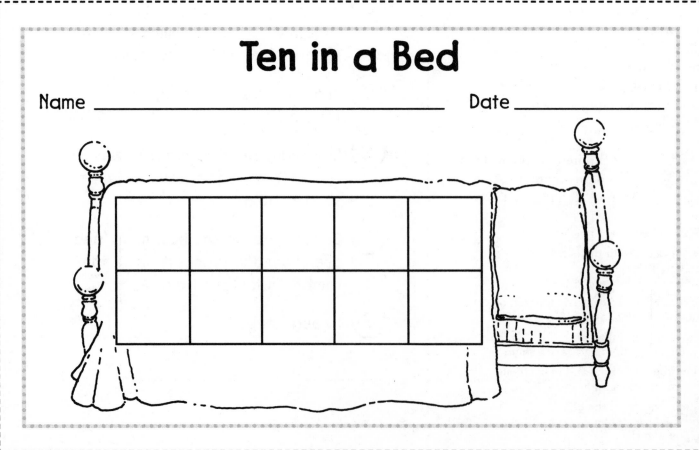

Shoe Box Learning Centers: Addition & Subtraction   Scholastic Teaching Resources

Ten in a Bed

Name _____ Date _____

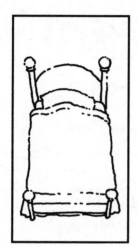 − 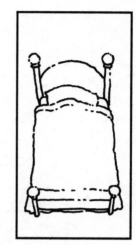 =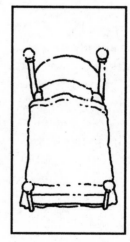

Ten in a Bed

Name _____ Date _____

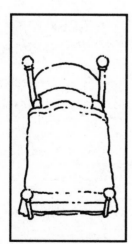 −  =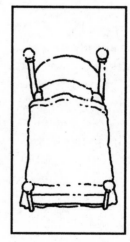

Candy Count

Children practice "counting on" while trying to get all the sums possible with the roll of two number cubes.

Materials

- shoe box
- box label
- student directions
- scissors
- glue
- game board (page 25)
- number cubes (numbers and dots)
- crayons

Shoe Box Setup

Make copies of the game board. Place the game boards, number cubes, and crayons inside the shoe box. Glue the label to one end of the box and the student directions to the inside of the lid.

TIP As a variation, have children share one game board, with each player using two different-colored crayons. Players who roll a number that is already colored in can roll again or let the play pass to the next player. Players can work together to color all the gumballs. To make a new game, white out the existing numbers on the gumballs and write in new ones. Make a new set of number and dot cubes that will add up to the new numbers on the game board.

Counting On

Candy Count

① ② ③ ④ ⑤

Directions
(for 2 or more players)

① Each player takes a game board. Take turns rolling both the number cube and the dot cube. Say the number on the number cube. Then count on the number of dots on the dot cube.

② Color in the gumball that shows the sum.

③ The first player to color in all the gumballs wins the game.

Candy Count

Name _____ Date _____

Give Me a Sign

Children determine whether a number fact is an addition or subtraction equation.

Materials

- shoe box
- box label
- student directions
- scissors
- glue
- Wikki Stix (available at craft stores)
- number card templates (page 13)
- marker

Shoe Box Setup

Cut the Wikki Stix into one-inch lengths. Write addition and subtraction facts on number card templates (or index cards), leaving out the plus or minus signs (but including the equal sign). Place the number fact cards and Wikki Stix inside the shoe box. Glue the label to one end of the box and the student directions to the inside of the lid.

TIP To vary the activity or create a companion shoe box center, cut longer pieces of Wikki Stix and make new index cards that have addition and subtraction facts with one number missing. Have students use the Wikki Stix to form the missing number on the index card.

Distinguishing Between Operations

Give Me a Sign

$-$ $+$
$+$
$-$ $=$
$+$

Directions

1. Choose a number fact card.

2. Use Wikki Stix to add a plus sign if it is an addition fact or a minus sign if it is a subtraction fact.

3. Choose another card and repeat.

Shoe Box Learning Centers: Addition & Subtraction   Scholastic Teaching Resources

Golfing for Numbers

In this game of golf, children add two-digit numbers and then compare sums to determine the winner.

Materials

- shoe box
- box label
- student directions
- scissors
- glue
- game board (page 28)
- number cubes
- pencils

Shoe Box Setup

Make copies of the game board. Place the game boards, number cubes, and pencils inside the shoe box. Glue the label to one end of the box and the student directions to the inside of the lid.

TIP **I**f the game is a tie, children can use calculators to add up their scores for all five holes to determine the winner.

Adding Two-Digit Numbers

Golfing for Numbers

Directions
(for 2 or more players)

1 Each player takes a game board. Take turns rolling a number cube. Go to the first hole on the game board. Write the number you roll on one of the golf balls.

2 Once each player has filled in the four golf balls at the first hole, add the pair of two-digit numbers.

3 The player with the lowest sum wins that hole. Play again to fill in the golf balls for each hole. The player with the lowest sum for the most holes wins the game.

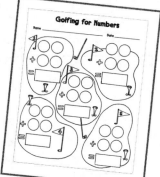

Golfing for Numbers

Name _____   Date _____

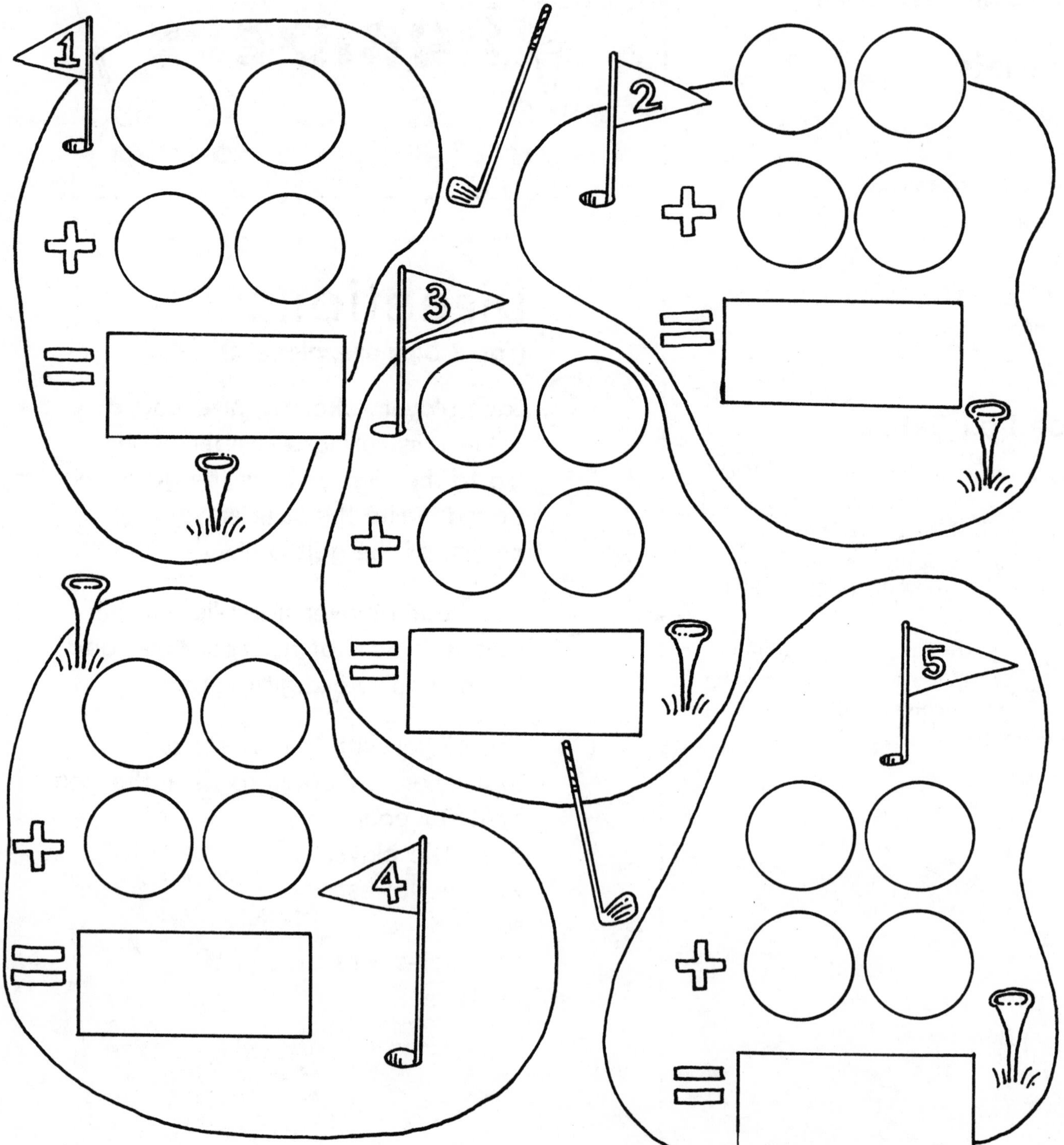

1

＋

＝

2

＋

＝

3

＋

＝

4

＝

5

＋

＝

Shoe Box Learning Centers: Addition & Subtraction · Scholastic Teaching Resources

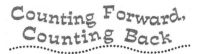

Through the Zoo

Children become familiar with the concepts of adding as counting forward and subtracting as counting back, as they make their way through a zoo.

Materials

- shoe box
- box label
- student directions
- scissors
- glue
- number card templates (page 13)
- marker
- game board (pages 30–31)
- plastic animals
- number cubes

Shoe Box Setup

Write plus and minus signs on number card templates (or index cards). Make a copy of the game board. Glue or tape the two game board pieces together as indicated. Place the cards, game board, animals, and number cubes inside the shoe box. Glue the label to one end of the box and the student directions to the inside of the lid.

TIP You may want to add to the shoe box plastic animals and people that children can arrange on the zoo game board before they play.

Counting Forward, Counting Back

Through the Zoo

Directions
(for 2 or more players)

(1) Choose an animal. Place it on Enter.

(2) Take turns rolling the number cube and picking a card. If you pick a plus sign move forward that number of spaces. If you pick a minus sign, move backward that number of spaces (but not past the beginning).

(3) The player who gets through the zoo first wins.

Through the Zoo

ENTER

The Number Quilt

Children create a colorful quilt as they practice adding combinations of three numbers that add up to 12.

Materials

- shoe box
- box label
- student directions
- scissors
- glue
- number quilt (page 33)
- number cubes
- pencils
- crayons

Shoe Box Setup

Make copies of the number quilt. Place the number quilts, number cubes, pencils, and crayons inside the shoe box. Glue the label to one end of the box and the student directions to the inside of the lid.

TIP To vary the game, have children try to complete a row that adds up to a number other than 12. Or have each child choose a different target number. Each child then tries to complete a row that adds up to that number.

Adding Three Numbers

The Number Quilt

Directions
(for 2 or more players)

1 Take turns rolling the number cube. Write the number rolled in one square of the quilt. Color in that square. (All players use the same game board.)

2 The first player to complete a row of three (in any direction) that adds up to 12 wins the game.

The Number Quilt

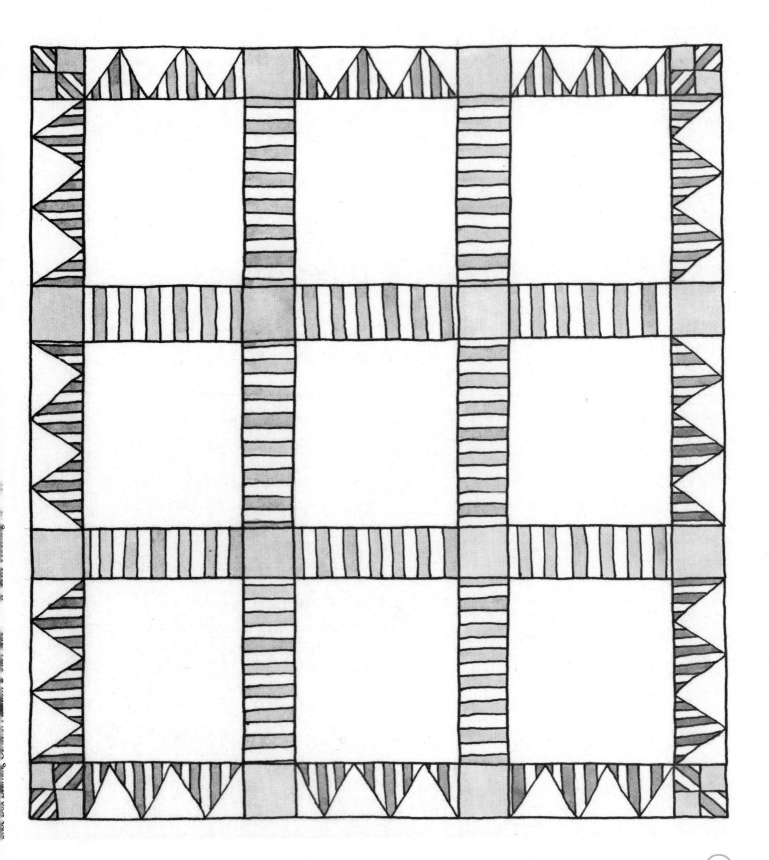

Subtraction Ribbon Boards

Children solve subtraction number problems by manipulating ribbons.

Materials

- shoe box
- box label
- student directions
- scissors
- glue
- cardboard squares (about 6 by 6 inches each)
- ribbon (several different colors or patterns)
- masking tape
- number card templates (page 13)
- marker
- pencils
- paper

Shoe Box Setup

Make several ribbon boards with different numbers of ribbons. Secure the ribbons to the boards by taping them across the top. Write subtraction number sentences on the card templates (or use index cards). Include the equal sign, but leave off the answer. Place the ribbon boards, number problem cards, pencils, and paper inside the shoe box. Glue the label to one end of the box and the student directions to the inside of the lid.

TIP Make ribbon boards available at your math table for children to use when solving pencil-and-paper math problems.

Solving Subtraction Problems

Subtraction Ribbon Boards

Directions

(1) Choose a number problem. Write it on a sheet of paper.

(2) Find the ribbon board that has the same number of ribbons as the first number in your number problem.

(3) Find the take-away number in your number problem. Lift that many ribbons from your ribbon board.

(4) Count how many ribbons are left.

(5) Write that number on your paper to complete the number sentence.

$10 - 4 =$

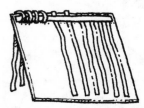

Shoe Box Learning Centers: Addition & Subtraction · Scholastic Teaching Resources

Big Snake, Little Snake

Children find the difference between two linking cube "snakes."

Materials

- shoe box
- box label
- student directions
- scissors
- glue
- number cards (page 11)
- record sheet (page 36)
- linking cubes (all one color)
- crayons (same color as linking cubes)
- pencils

Shoe Box Setup

Make copies of the number cards and record sheet. Cut apart the number cards. Place the number cards, record sheets, linking cubes, crayons, and pencils inside the shoe box. Glue the label to one end of the box and the student directions to the inside of the lid.

TIP Tell children that snakes often coil their bodies, making them appear shorter than they really are. To let children explore this idea, cut lengths of string, some longer than others. Coil some of the strings; leave others stretched out. Let children guess the order of the snakes from shortest to longest. Then measure to find out the actual order.

Finding the Difference

Big Snake, Little Snake

Directions

(1) Choose two number cards. Use the linking cubes to build a "snake" that equals each number.

(2) Place the snakes on the record sheet. Which snake is bigger? To find out how much bigger, count how many more parts one snake has than the other.

(3) Record the difference. Make a record of each snake by coloring in the number of cubes for each.

(4) Write the subtraction number sentence that tells about your picture.

(5) Choose two more cards and repeat.

Big Snake, Little Snake

Name _____

Date _____

A

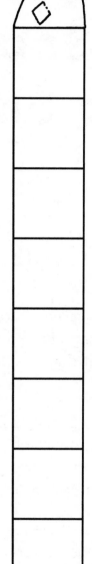

B

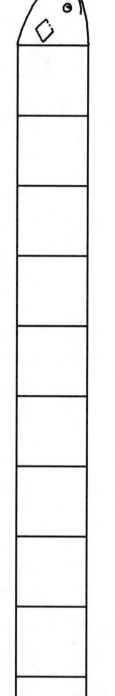

Which snake is bigger? _____

The difference is _____

_____ − _____ = _____ .

Shoe Box Learning Centers: Addition & Subtraction   Scholastic Teaching Resources

Spot the Facts

Children "spot" fact families on ladybugs.

Materials

- shoe box
- box label
- student directions
- scissors
- glue
- ladybug patterns (page 38)
- record sheets (page 39)
- pencils

Shoe Box Setup

Copy the ladybug patterns onto card stock. Add dots to represent different fact families. Make copies of the record sheets and cut apart. Place the ladybugs, record sheets, and pencils inside the shoe box. Glue the label to one end of the box and the student directions to the inside of the lid.

TIP Instead of drawing the dots, you can use self-adhesive dots. As a variation, reverse the activity. Record number sentences on index cards and have students use bingo chips to give the ladybug the corresponding number of dots.

Writing Fact Families

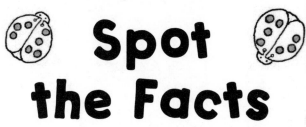

Spot the Facts

Directions

1) Choose a ladybug. Count the spots. Draw them on the record sheet.

2) Write two addition and two subtraction number sentences to go with your picture.

3) Choose a new ladybug and repeat.

Spot the Facts

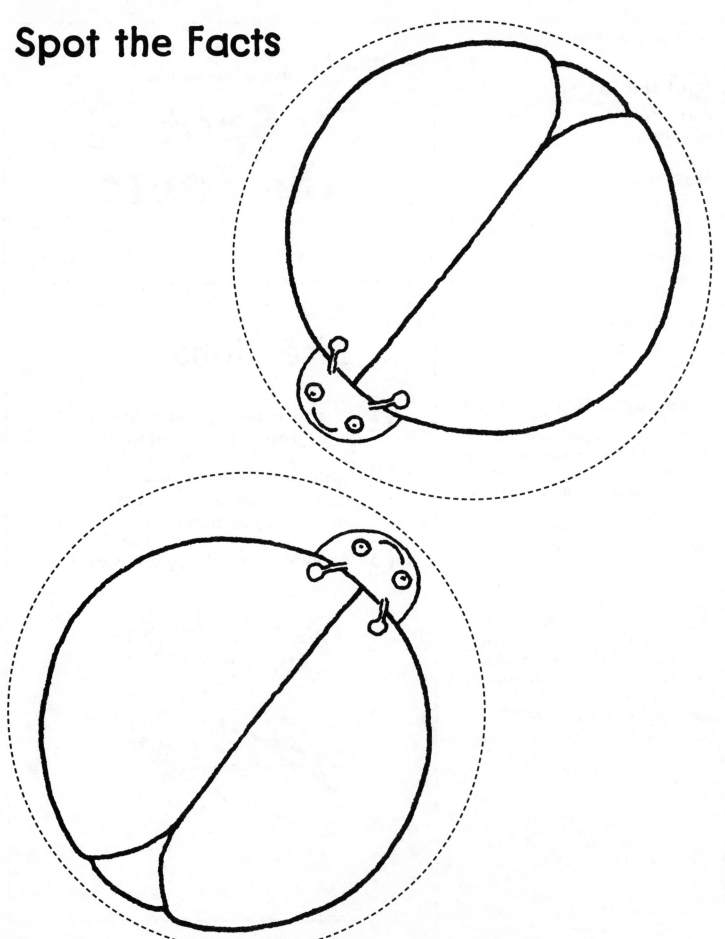

Spot the Facts

Name _____ Date _____

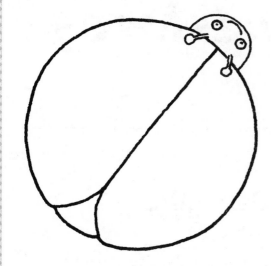

_____

_____

_____

_____

Spot the Facts

Name _____ Date _____

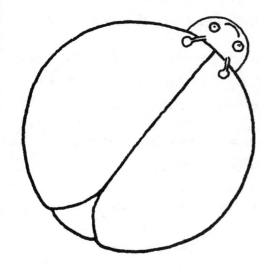

_____

_____

_____

_____

Ten Frame Take-Away

Children subtract two-digit numbers using beans and ten frames.

Materials

- shoe box
- box label
- student directions
- scissors
- glue
- card stock
- two sets of number cards 1–9 (page 11)
- ten frames and record sheet (page 41)
- dried beans
- pencils

Shoe Box Setup

Make place-value boards by creating two columns labeled "Tens" and "Ones" on sheets of card stock. Make copies of and cut apart the number cards, ten frames, and record sheets. Place the number cards, ten frames, record sheets, beans, and pencils inside the shoe box. Glue the label to one end of the box and the student directions to the inside of the lid.

TIP As a variation, use this same shoe box to have children practice adding two-digit numbers. Modify the directions and record sheet to reflect this change.

Understanding Place Value

Ten Frame Take-Away

Directions

1. Choose four cards. Use them to make two two-digit numbers on the place-value board. Place the larger number on top.

2. Read the number on top. Count it out using beans and ten frames.

3. Read the number on the bottom. Remove that many beans from the ten frames. Regroup if you need to.

4. Find the difference between the two numbers by counting the number of beans left on the ten frames.

5. Record the subtraction equation on the record sheet.

6. Try again with new numbers.

Ten Frame Take-Away

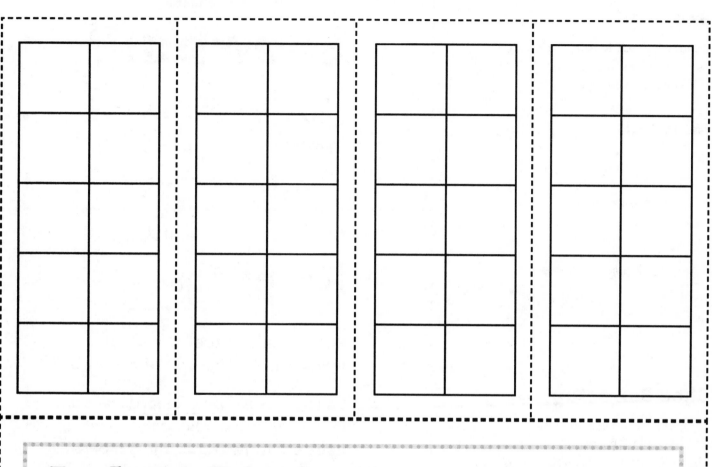

Ten Frame Take-Away
Place-Value Board

Name _____

Date _____

Tens   Ones

Shoe Box Centers: Addition and Subtraction   Scholastic Teaching Resources

Snowball!

Children watch their numbers "snowball" as they double the number rolled again and again.

Materials

- shoe box
- box label
- student directions
- scissors
- glue
- snowball record sheets (page 43)
- number cubes
- counters
- pencils

Shoe Box Setup

Make copies of and cut apart the snowball patterns. Place the snowball patterns, number cubes, counters, and pencils inside the shoe box. Glue the label to one end of the box and the student directions to the inside of the lid.

TIP As a variation, have children roll a new number each time and compute the sums as they go along. How "big" a snowball can they make?

Doubling Numbers

Snowball!

Directions

(1) Roll a number cube. Write that number in the top box of a snowball.

(2) Double this number. Record the sum in the next box. You can use the counters to help add the numbers.

(3) Double the previous number to fill all the boxes.

(4) Roll a new number. Make a new snowball.

Shoe Box Learning Centers: Addition & Subtraction   Scholastic Teaching Resources

Snowball!

Name _____

Date _____

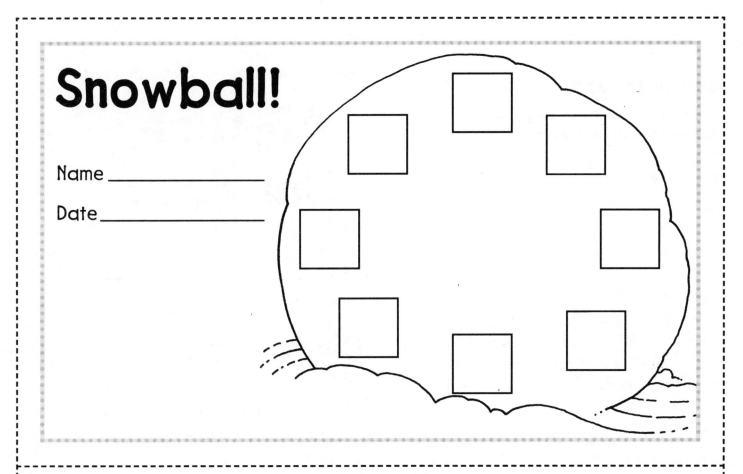

Snowball!

Name _____

Date _____

Shoe Box Learning Centers: Addition & Subtraction   Scholastic Teaching Resources

Picture the Fact

Children use rubber stamp designs to illustrate addition and subtraction facts.

Materials

- shoe box
- box label
- student directions
- scissors
- glue
- number card templates (page 13)
- marker
- addition and subtraction record sheets (page 45)
- rubber stamps
- ink pads
- crayons

Shoe Box Setup

Write addition and subtraction number facts on the card templates (or index cards). Make copies of both record sheets and cut apart. Place the number facts, record sheets, rubber stamps, ink pads, and crayons inside the shoe box. Glue the label to one end of the box and the student directions to the inside of the lid.

TIP To take the activity further, have children create fact family books by stamping designs for facts in the same family. Staple pages together and add a cover with a stamped design border. If rubber stamps are not available, have children draw the pictures using crayons.

Representing Addition and Subtraction Facts

$$8 - 3 = 5$$

Picture the Fact

$$8 + 3 = 11$$

Directions

① Choose a number fact. Find the record sheet that goes with your number fact (+ or −).

② Write the number fact on the record sheet. If it is an addition fact, stamp designs for each addend. If it is a subtraction fact, stamp designs for the largest number in the first box. Then use a crayon to cross off the amount taken away.

③ Stamp designs to show the sum or difference.

Picture the Fact: Addition

Name _____ Date _____

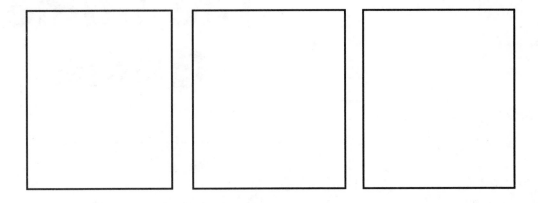

\+ _____ = _____

Picture the Fact: Subtraction

Name _____ Date _____

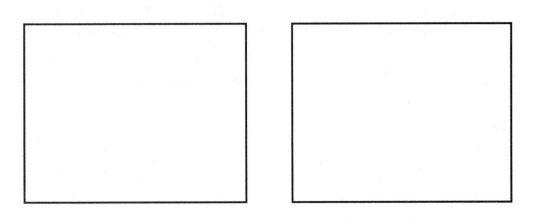

− _____ = _____

The Name Game

In this game, children practice naming a number in different ways.

Materials

- shoe box
- box label
- student directions
- scissors
- glue
- record sheets (page 47)
- number cards (pages 11–12)
- egg timer
- name tags
- pencils

Shoe Box Setup

Make copies of and cut apart the record sheets and number cards. Place the record sheets, number cards, egg timer, name tags, and pencils inside the shoe box. Glue the label to one end of the box and the student directions to the inside of the lid.

TIP **I**ntroduce this activity during calendar time and have children suggest different ways to name the date. For a cooperative version, have children count up how many different ways they found all together to name the number.

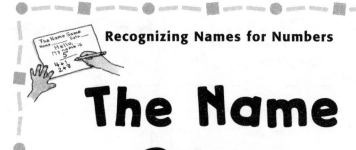

Recognizing Names for Numbers

The Name Game

Directions
(for 2 or more players)

(1) Choose one number from the stack of number cards. Each player writes that number on a name tag.

(2) Turn over the timer. Then each player records different names for that number on the name tag.

(3) When the time has run out, players share their ways of showing the number. The player with the most correct ways not recorded by any other player wins.

The Name Game

Name _____ Date _____

Hello,
My name is

_____

The Name Game

Name _____ Date _____

Hello,
My name is

_____

Seeing Double

Children explore doubles by completing a mini-book of addition facts.

Materials

- shoe box
- box label
- student directions
- scissors
- glue
- mini-book pages (pages 49–54)
- crayons
- pencils

Shoe Box Setup

Make copies of the mini-book pages. Cut apart the pages and staple to bind. Place the mini-books, crayons, and pencils inside the shoe box. Glue the label to one end of the box and the student directions to the inside of the lid.

TIP Send home the mini-books with a letter asking parents to help their children learn the "doubles" facts. Then teach children to use doubles as a strategy to figure out "almost doubles," such as 2 + 3 = 5 (an "almost double" for 2 + 2 or 3 + 3).

Identifying Doubles Facts

Seeing Double

Directions

① Take a mini-book.
Write your name on the cover.

② Complete each picture to match the number sentence. Color in the pictures.

③ Create your own doubles picture on the last page.

Seeing Double

Create your own doubles picture.

_____ + _____ = _____

12

1 + = 2

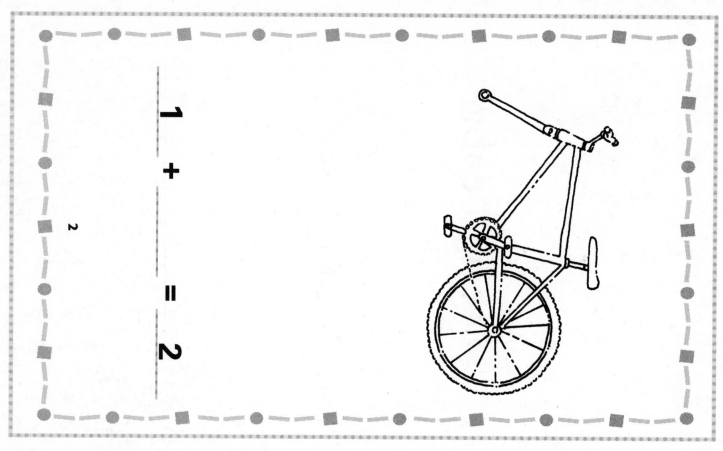

2

2 + = 4

3

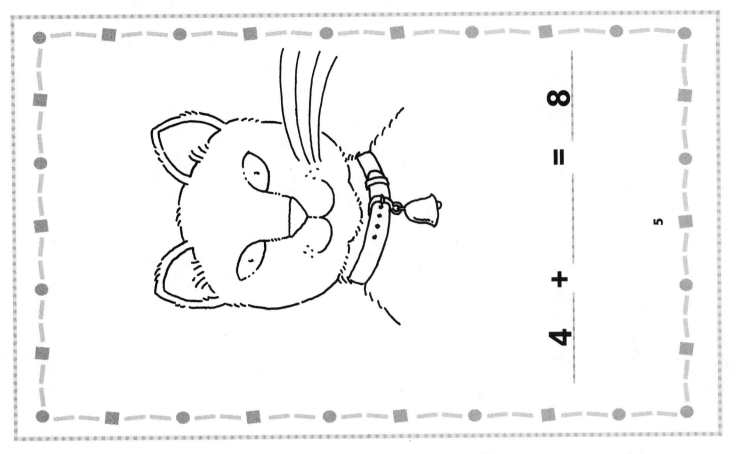

$4 + \underline{} = 8$

5

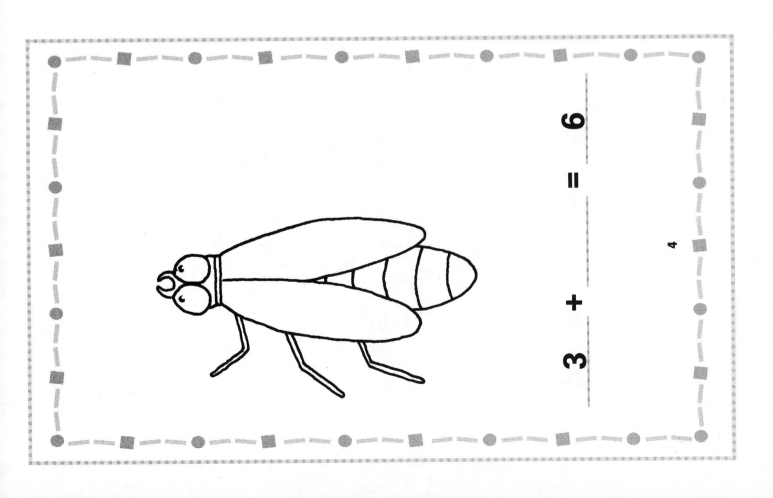

$3 + \underline{} = 6$

4

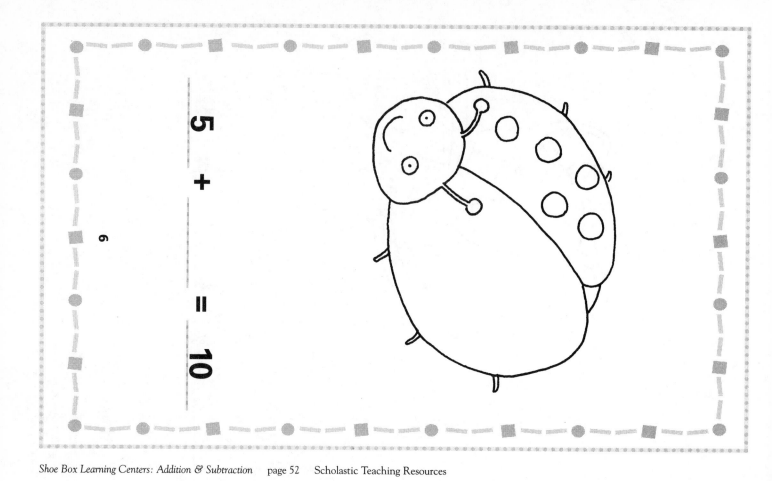

5 + _____ = 10

6

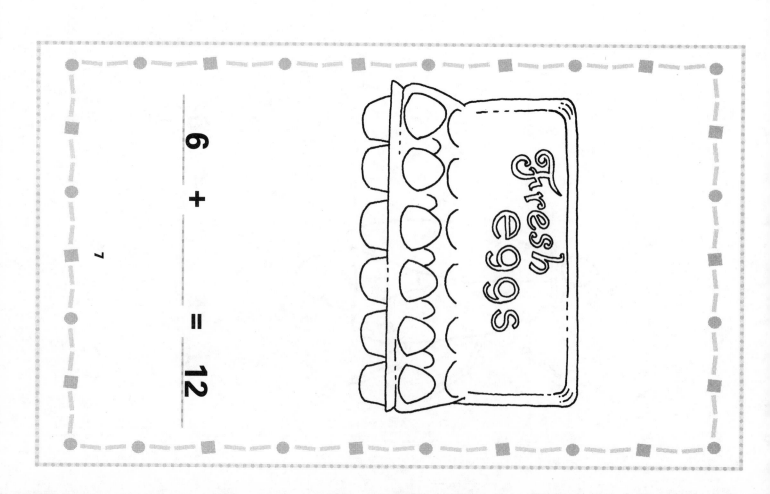

6 + _____ = 12

7

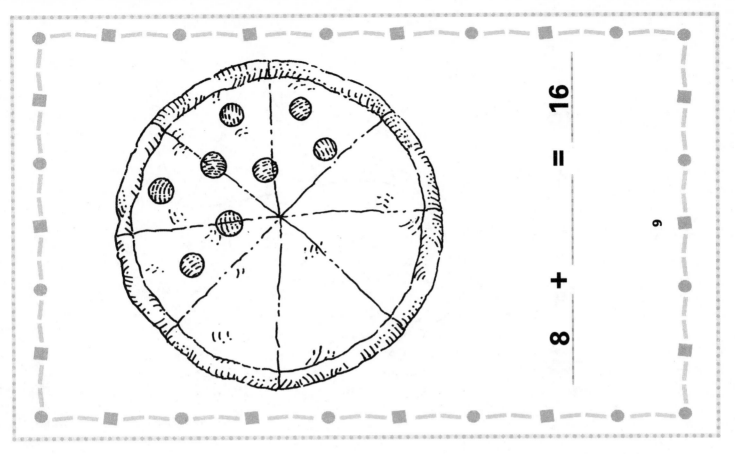

8 + 9 = 16

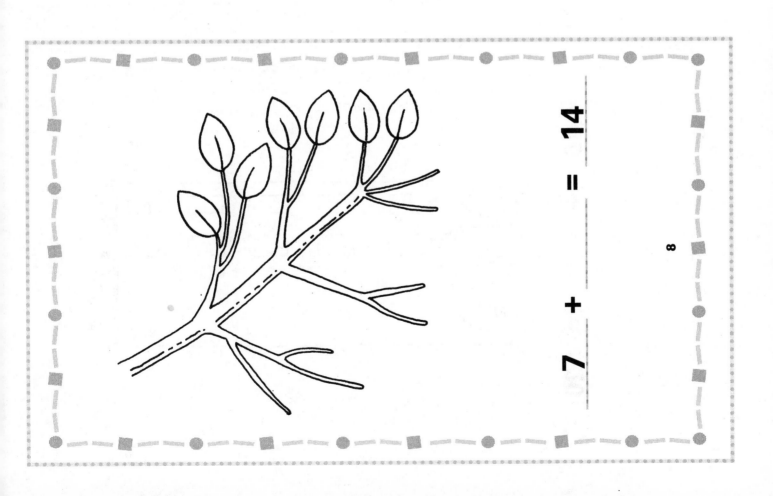

7 + 8 = 14

9 + = 18

10

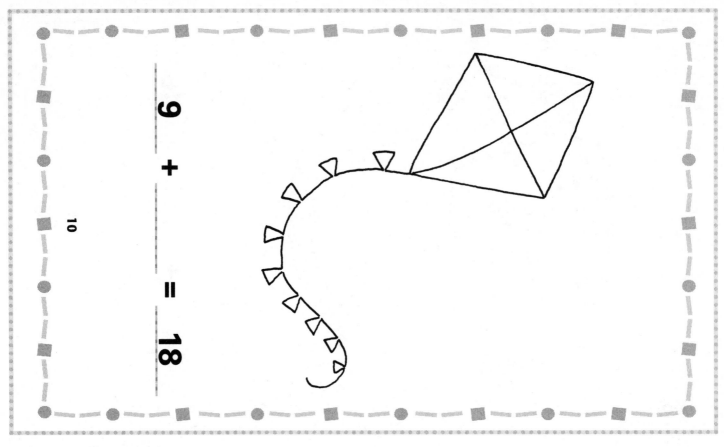

10 + = 20

11

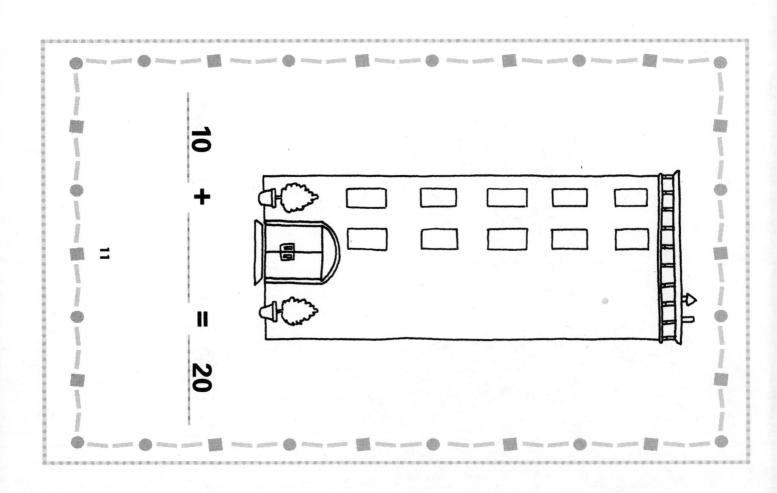

Doubles Addition

Students learn about the properties of doubles by exploring the mirror image of objects.

Materials

- shoe box
- box label
- student directions
- scissors
- glue
- record sheets (page 56)
- small objects (such as jacks, toy cars and animals, buttons, and marbles)
- small mirrors
- pencils

Shoe Box Setup

Make copies of the record sheets and cut apart. Place the record sheets, objects, mirrors, and pencils inside the shoe box. Glue the label to one end of the box and the student directions to the inside of the lid.

TIP Share a Chinese folktale to learn more about the magic of doubles. *Two of Everything*, by Lily Toy Hong (Whitman, 1993), tells the story of an elderly couple who find a pot that magically doubles everything they put into it—including the wife, who accidentally falls in!

Exploring Doubles Facts

 # Doubles Addition

Directions

1. Choose several objects. Draw a picture of your objects in the first box.

2. Hold up the mirror to the objects, as shown:

3. Draw a picture of what you see in the mirror.

4. Write a number sentence to show how many objects are on the table and in the mirror.

$$2 + 2 = 4$$

Doubles Addition

Name _____ Date _____

Box	Mirror

_____ + _____ = _____

Doubles Addition

Name _____ Date _____

Box	Mirror

_____ + _____ = _____

Shoe Box Learning Centers: Addition & Subtraction   Scholastic Teaching Resources

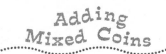

Pocket Money

Children determine the amount of "pocket money" by adding mixed coins.

Materials

- shoe box
- box label
- student directions
- scissors
- glue
- record sheets (page 58)
- coins (quarters, dimes, nickels, and pennies)
- film canisters
- number cubes
- pockets (cut from old pants)
- pencils

Shoe Box Setup

Make copies of and cut apart the record sheets. Place each type of coin in a film canister. Label the canisters. Place the record sheets, canisters, number cubes, pockets, and pencils inside the shoe box. Glue the label to one end of the box and the student directions to the inside of the lid.

TIP **I**nstead of cutting pockets from old pants, try making them by stapling together two pocket-size pieces of craft foam or felt. To take the activity further, have children use the back of the record sheet to record other combinations of coins that equal the same amount as in one of the pockets. Have them draw the coins to show their answers.

Adding Mixed Coins

Pocket Money

Directions

1 Roll a number cube. Record that number in the "Quarters" column. Take that number of quarters and place them in the pocket.

2 Repeat step 1 for dimes, nickels, and pennies.

3 Empty the pocket and add up the value of the coins. Write the total amount on the record sheet.

4 Follow the same steps to complete the record sheet. Circle the pocket that had the most money.

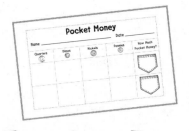

Pocket Money

Name _____ Date _____

Quarters	Dimes	Nickels	Pennies	How Much Pocket Money?

Pocket Money

Name _____ Date _____

Quarters	Dimes	Nickels	Pennies	How Much Pocket Money?

Shoe Box Learning Centers: Addition and Subtraction   Scholastic Teaching Resources

Spill the Beans

Children practice identifying and recording number combinations for several fact families.

Materials

- shoe box
- box label
- student directions
- scissors
- glue
- dried white beans
- blue spray paint
- cup
- record sheet (page 60)
- number cards 2–10 (page 11)
- pencils

Shoe Box Setup

Spray paint one side of the beans. Make copies of the record sheet and number cards. Cut apart the number cards. Place the beans, number cards, record sheets, and pencils inside the box. Glue the label to one end of the box and the student directions to the inside of the lid.

TIP Once children have "spilled the beans" for each fact family, let them staple the pages together to create a take-home book. Encourage families to work with children to help them learn their facts.

Recording Number Combinations

Spill the Beans

Directions

(1) Choose a number card. Write that number on the record sheet. Take that number of beans.

(2) Place the beans in the cup. Shake the beans and spill them onto your workspace.

(3) Record the number of beans that land blue side up. Record the number of beans that land white side up.

(4) Repeat until you find all the number facts for your family. (The number of facts for each number family will be equal to your number + 1.)

(5) Choose a new card and repeat.

Spill the Beans

Name _____ Date _____

Number Family _____

Blue	+	White	=	Total

Shoe Box Learning Centers: Addition & Subtraction   Scholastic Teaching Resources

Number Train

Children form number sentences using six numbers chosen at random.

Materials

- shoe box
- box label
- student directions
- scissors
- glue
- number cards 1–20 (pages 11–12)
- record sheet (page 62)
- pencils

Shoe Box Setup

Cut apart the number cards. Make copies of the record sheet. Place the number cards, record sheets, and pencils inside the shoe box. Glue the label to one end of the box and the student directions to the inside of the lid.

TIP As a challenge, encourage children to try to make number sentences that involve adding three numbers.

Writing Number Sentences

Number Train

Directions

① Choose six number cards. Write each number in a boxcar on the record sheet.

② Using those numbers, make as many addition and subtraction number sentences (for example, 7 – 4 = 3) as you can. You don't need to use all of your numbers, but each part of your number sentence must be on the train. Write each number sentence on a line below the number train.

③ Choose new numbers and repeat.

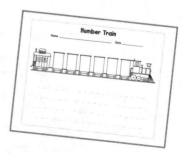

Number Train

Name _____

Date _____

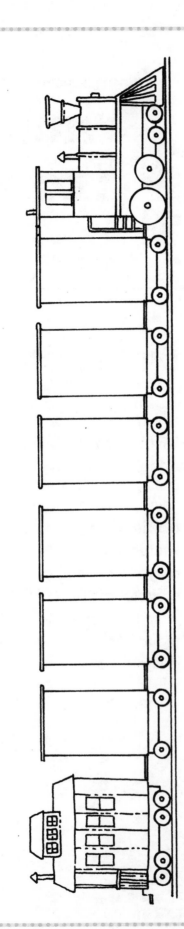

Shoe Box Learning Centers: Addition & Subtraction   Scholastic Teaching Resources

Polka-Dot Pajamas

Children add polka dots to plain pajamas to illustrate number sentences.

Materials

- shoe box
- box label
- student directions
- scissors
- glue
- number card templates (page 13)
- record sheets (page 64)
- stamper markers (two different colors)

Shoe Box Setup

Write number sentences on card templates (or index cards). Make copies of and cut apart the record sheets. Place number sentences, record sheets, and markers inside the shoe box. Glue the label to one end of the box and the student directions to the inside of the lid.

TIP **C**hildren can staple their polka-dot pajama pages together to create take-home books to share with their families.

Representing Addition Facts

Polka-Dot Pajamas

Directions

(1) Choose a number sentence. Write it on the record sheet.

(2) Stamp polka dots on the pajamas to go with the number sentence. Use two different colors. Draw the face.

(3) Choose a new number sentence and repeat.

Polka-Dot Pajamas

Name _____

Date _____

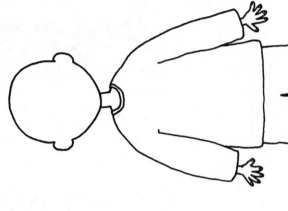

+ ___ = ___

Polka-Dot Pajamas

Name _____

Date _____

+ ___ = ___

Shoe Box Learning Centers: Addition & Subtraction Scholastic Teaching Resources

Pattern Block Pets

Children use pattern block shapes with assigned money values to find the cost of an animal they've created.

Materials

- shoe box
- box label
- student directions
- scissors
- glue
- record sheet (page 66)
- pattern blocks
- crayons
- pencils

Shoe Box Setup

Make copies of the record sheet. Place the record sheets, pattern blocks, crayons, and pencils inside the shoe box. Glue the label to one end of the box and the student directions to the inside of the lid.

TIP As an extension, have children compare the cost of their pets. Ask: *Which one is most expensive? Which one is least expensive? How much more is one pet than another?*

Using Addition to Solve Problems

Pattern Block Pets

Directions

(1) Use the pattern block shapes to make an animal. You can use each shape more than once.

(2) On the record sheet, color squares to show how many of each shape you used.

(3) Use the value of each block to find the cost of your pet. Record the amount on the price tag.

(4) Make another animal and repeat.

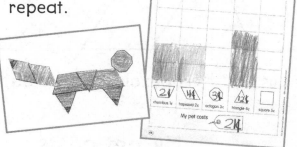

Pattern Block Pets

Name _____ Date _____

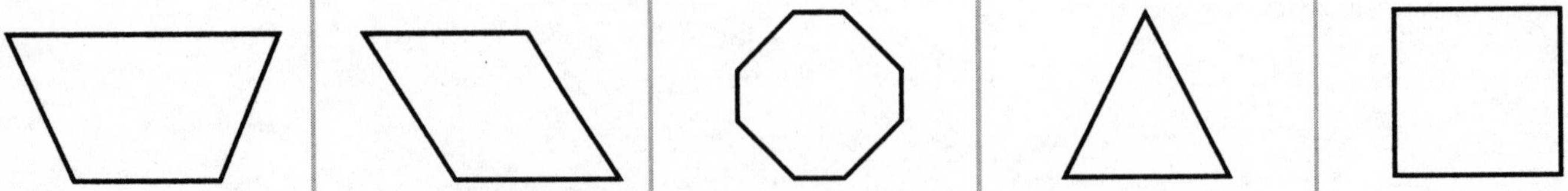

rhombus 1¢	trapezoid 2¢	octagon 3¢	triangle 4¢	square 5¢

My pet costs

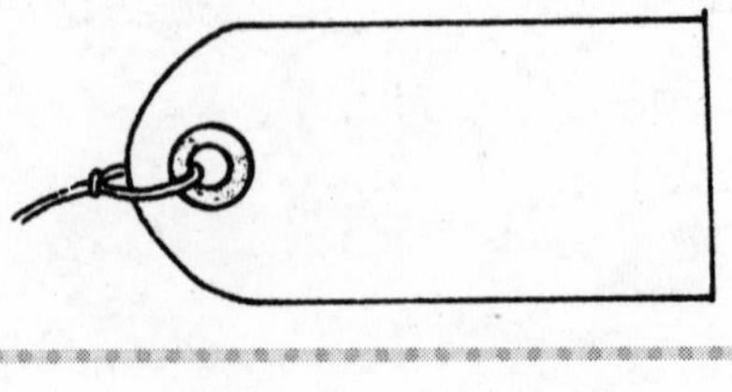

Seed Stories

Children solve story problems using a math mat and manipulatives.

Materials

- shoe box
- box label
- student directions
- scissors
- glue
- math mat (page 68)
- story cards (page 69)
- sunflower seeds
- paper
- pencils

Shoe Box Setup

Make copies of the math mat and story cards. Place the math mats, story cards, seeds, paper, and pencils inside the shoe box. Glue the label to one end of the box and the student directions to the inside of the lid.

TIP **I**nvite children to create their own story cards when they are finished. They can trade story cards with each other and use the seeds and math mat to solve them.

Solving Story Problems

Seed Stories

Directions

1 Choose a story card.

2 Use the seeds and math mat to solve the number problem.

3 Write the card number and the answer on your paper.

4 Choose another story card and repeat.

The 🌻 has 5 seeds.
The 🐦 has 8 seeds.
How many more seeds does the 🐦 have?

The 🌻 has 4 seeds.
The 🐦 has 3 seeds.
How many seeds do they have all together?

Seed Stories

Seed Stories

Seed Stories

①
The 🌻 has 5 seeds.
The 🐦 has 8 seeds.
How many more seeds does
the 🐦 have?

②
The 🌻 has 4 seeds.
The 🐦 has 3 seeds.
How many seeds do they have
all together?

③
The 🌻 has 6 seeds. The
🐦 has 3 more seeds
than the 🌻. How many
seeds does the 🐦 have?

④
The 🐦 has 9 seeds.
The 🌻 has 4 fewer seeds.
How many seeds does the
🌻 have?

⑤
There are 10 seeds all
together. If the 🐦
has 2, how many seeds
does the 🌻 have?

⑥
The 🌻 has 8 seeds.
The 🐦 has half as many.
How many seeds does the
🐦 have?

⑦
The 🌻 has 5 seeds.
The 🐦 has twice as many.
How many seeds does the
🐦 have?

⑧
There are 12 seeds. The 🌻
and the 🐦 have the same
amount. How many seeds do
they each have?

Scrambled Eggs

Children see how quickly they can match number problems to their answers.

Materials

- shoe box
- box label
- student directions
- scissors
- glue
- plastic eggs (all one color)
- marker
- digital timer

Shoe Box Setup

Separate each egg. Write a number fact on one half of each egg and the answer on the other. Place the egg halves and timer inside the shoe box. Glue the label to one end of the box and the student directions to the inside of the lid.

TIP Turn this activity into a game: Give each child four egg halves. Place the remaining egg halves in a paper bag. Have children take turns choosing an egg half from the bag. If the egg matches one of theirs, they put the egg together. If not, it goes in a pile in the center. Players may choose from either the pile or the bag on each turn. The first player to rebuild all four eggs wins.

Scrambled Eggs

7-5   2

Directions

1. Set the timer.

2. Put the eggs back together by matching the problems to the answers.

3. Check the time.

4. Take the eggs apart and repeat. Try to beat your time.

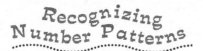

Name the Pattern

Children make and identify number patterns after re-creating them on a hundred board.

Materials

- shoe box
- box label
- student directions
- scissors
- glue
- hundred board (page 72)
- record sheet (page 73)
- bingo chips
- pencils

Shoe Box Setup

Make copies of the hundred board and record sheet. Place the hundred boards, record sheets, bingo chips, and pencils inside the shoe box. Glue the label to one end of the box and the student directions to the inside of the lid.

 TIP Reverse the activity by giving children the rule (for example, "minus 3") and having them create a pattern to go with it.

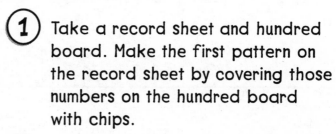

Recognizing Number Patterns

Name the Pattern

2 4 6 8

Directions

1 Take a record sheet and hundred board. Make the first pattern on the record sheet by covering those numbers on the hundred board with chips.

2 Name the pattern (for example, "plus 2" or "minus 5"). Write it on the record sheet.

3 Make the next pattern and repeat.

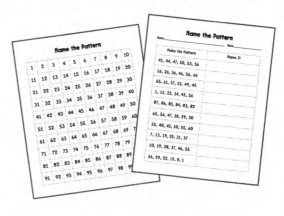

Name the Pattern

1	2	3	4	5	6	7	8	9	10
11	12	13	14	15	16	17	18	19	20
21	22	23	24	25	26	27	28	29	30
31	32	33	34	35	36	37	38	39	40
41	42	43	44	45	46	47	48	49	50
51	52	53	54	55	56	57	58	59	60
61	62	63	64	65	66	67	68	69	70
71	72	73	74	75	76	77	78	79	80
81	82	83	84	85	86	87	88	89	90
91	92	93	94	95	96	97	98	99	100

Sky-Box Learning Centers: Addition & Subtraction • Scholastic Teaching Resources

Name the Pattern

Name_____ Date _____

Make the Pattern	Name It
41, 44, 47, 50, 53, 56	
16, 26, 36, 46, 56, 66	
65, 61, 57, 53, 49, 45	
1, 12, 23, 34, 45, 56	
87, 86, 85, 84, 83, 82	
65, 56, 47, 38, 29, 20	
35, 40, 45, 50, 55, 60	
7, 13, 19, 25, 31, 37	
10, 19, 28, 37, 46, 55	
36, 29, 22, 15, 8, 1	

Mystery Number Blocks

Children find the numerical value of different-colored blocks using addition and subtraction clue cards.

Materials

- shoe box
- box label
- student directions
- scissors
- glue
- clue cards (page 75)
- record sheets (page 76)
- interlocking blocks (red, blue, yellow, and green)
- crayons
- pencils

Shoe Box Setup

Make copies of and cut apart the clue cards and record sheets. Place the clue cards, record sheets, blocks, crayons, and pencils inside the shoe box. Glue the label to one end of the box and the student directions to the inside of the lid.

TIP Challenge children to create their own clue cards for others to use.

Using Addition and Subtraction to Solve Problems

Mystery Number Blocks

Directions

① Choose a clue card. Write the number of the card at the top of the record sheet.

② Read the first clue. Find the value of each block. Place a block on each matching number on the record sheet.

③ Remove the blocks and color in each space with the matching crayon.

④ Choose a new card and repeat.

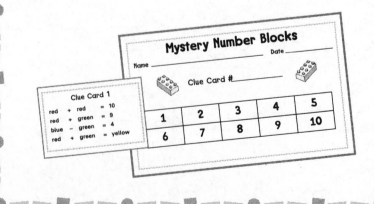

Mystery Number Blocks

Name _____ Date _____

Clue Card # _____

| 1 | 2 | 3 | 4 | 5 |
| 6 | 7 | 8 | 9 | 10 |

Clue Card 1

red + red = 10
red + green = 9
blue − green = 4
red + green = yellow

Mystery Number Blocks

Clue Card 1

red	+	red	= 10
red	+	green	= 9
blue	–	green	= 4
red	+	green	= yellow

Clue Card 2

red	+	red	= 2
blue	+	red	= 4
yellow	–	blue	= 1
yellow	+	red	= green

Clue Card 3

green	+	green	= 8
blue	+	green	= 10
yellow	–	blue	= 5
blue	+	red	= yellow

Clue Card 4

green	+	green	= 2
blue	–	green	= 4
blue	+	yellow	= 7
red	–	blue	= yellow

Clue Card 5

blue	+	blue	= 4
red	–	blue	= 1
yellow	–	red	= 6
yellow	–	blue	= green

Clue Card 6

blue	+	blue	= 12
blue	+	red	= 9
yellow	–	blue	= 3
yellow	+	red	= green

Clue Card 7

yellow	+	yellow	= 6
green	–	yellow	= 5
green	–	red	= 7
green	+	red	= blue

Clue Card 8

yellow	+	yellow	= 4
red	–	yellow	= 5
green	+	red	= 8
blue	–	green	= red

Mystery Number Blocks

Name _____ Date _____

 Clue Card #_____

1	2	3	4	5
6	7	8	9	10

Mystery Number Blocks

Name _____ Date _____

 Clue Card #_____

1	2	3	4	5
6	7	8	9	10

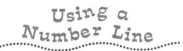
Hop to It!

Children practice using a number line to solve addition and subtraction problems.

Materials

- shoe box
- box label
- student directions
- scissors
- glue
- number line (page 78)
- number card templates (page 13)
- small plastic animals (for example, frog, kangaroo, grasshopper, rabbit)
- marker

Shoe Box Setup

Cut apart the number line strips. Tape or glue the strips together in numerical order. Write addition and subtraction facts on number card templates (or index cards) with the answers written on the back. Place the animals, number lines, and cards inside the shoe box. Glue the label to one end of the box and the student directions to the inside of the lid.

TIP Introduce this activity by sharing the book *Who Hops?*, by Katie Davis (Voyager, 2001). Before reading, invite children to guess which animals hop.

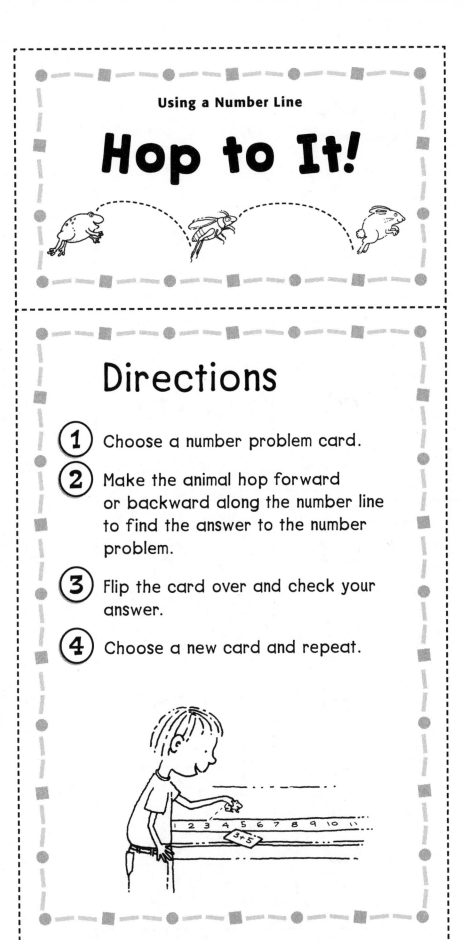

Using a Number Line

Hop to It!

Directions

1. Choose a number problem card.

2. Make the animal hop forward or backward along the number line to find the answer to the number problem.

3. Flip the card over and check your answer.

4. Choose a new card and repeat.

Hop to It!

5
4
3
2
1
0

10
9
8
7
6

15
14
13
12
11

20
19
18
17
16

More Easy-to-Make Shoe Box Learning Centers

Add to your supply of shoe box centers periodically by creating fresh activities to keep student interest strong. Following are more ideas for making shoe box centers that reinforce addition and subtraction skills. For each, use the reproducible templates (right) to make a label and write student directions. Glue the label to the outside of the box and the student directions to the inside of the lid.

Subtraction Stacks

Children use manipulatives to represent numbers and then compare to see how those numbers relate.

Stock a shoe box with number cards (pages 11–12), linking cubes, centimeter or 1/2-inch grid paper, pencils, and crayons. Instruct students to choose two number cards and make stacks of cubes to equal those numbers. Have them find the difference by counting how many more cubes one stack has than the other. Ask children to make a record of the stacks by coloring in the number of cubes for each. Then have them write the subtraction number sentence that tells about their picture.

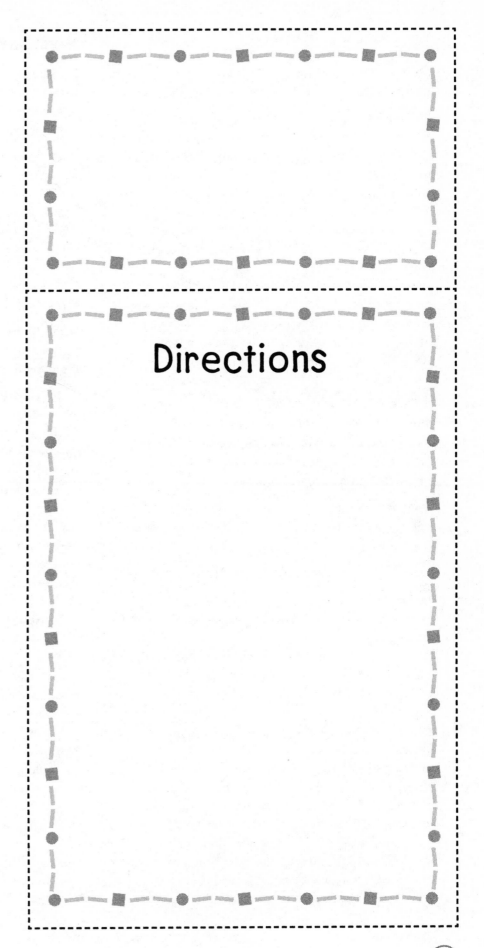

Directions

Race to 100

Here's a game that lets children practice computation skills as they try to be the first to reach 100.

Stock a shoe box with number cubes, paper, and pencils. Have each player take a number cube and place it with the "1" facing up. One at a time, players turn, not roll, the number cube in any direction and record the number on a sheet of paper. Players add their numbers as they go along. The first player to reach exactly 100 wins the game. If players go over 100, they may subtract or add the numbers as they wish to attempt to reach exactly 100. As a variation, have students play the game in reverse, starting at 100 and subtracting numbers to reach 0.

Target Addition

This fun game lets children toss a marker (such as a penny) on a target to practice strategies for adding whole numbers and understanding how numbers relate to one another.

To make a target, cut a sheet of sturdy paper into a large triangle (no longer at the base than the length of the shoe box). Draw colorful lines to divide the 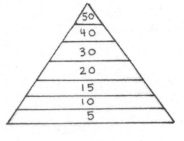 triangle horizontally into seven strips as shown. Label each strip from the base to the tip as follows: 5, 10, 15, 20, 30, 40, 50. Roll up the target, and place it, along with sticky tack, a penny (or other marker), paper, and pencils in the shoe box. Have children unroll the target and use sticky tack to secure the target to the floor or table space. To play, children take turns tossing the penny on the target and recording the number it lands on. (If the penny lands on a line, children can try again.) Children play for a set number of rounds, adding their scores as they go. How high can they go? As a variation, children can play with the goal of achieving the lowest score of all players.

Number Sentence Stories

Encourage mathematical communication with a shoe box center that combines math skills with writing.

Write number sentences on index cards (for example, 3 + 7 = 10). Place the number sentences, a small white board, wet-erase pen, and paper towels in the shoe box. Have children choose a number sentence and then write a brief story about it. Let children share their stories before erasing the board for the next child.

Clip-On Addition

Strengthen understanding of addition with an activity that lets children clip on clothespins to show the missing addend of a number fact.

Write equations on index cards. Leave a blank on each card for one of the addends. Stock a shoe box with the cards and a bag of clothespins. Have students choose a number fact card and then clip clothespins onto the card to show the missing addend. They can repeat the process using other cards. To make this activity self-checking, write the missing addend on the back of each card.  To extend the activity, have pairs of children take turns filling in missing addends and then telling stories about the numbers—for example, to go with the equation 7 + 3 = 10, a child might say, "Our birthday graph shows that seven kids have a birthday next month and three kids have a birthday the month after that. So ten kids have a birthday in the next two months."